anythin

1,000-YEAR-OLD SPONGES!

By Joni Kelly

Gareth Stevens
PUBLISHING

Please visit our website, www.garethstevens.com. For a free color catalog of all our high-quality books, call toll free 1-800-542-2595 or fax 1-877-542-2596.

Library of Congress Cataloging-in-Publication Data

Names: Kelly, Joni, author.
Title: 1,000-year-old sponges! / Joni Kelly.
Other titles: One thousand year old sponges
Description: New York : Gareth Stevens Publishing, [2019] | Series: World's longest-living animals | Includes index.
Identifiers: LCCN 2017029008| ISBN 9781538216989 (pbk.) | ISBN 9781538216996 (6 pack) | ISBN 9781538216972 (library bound)
Subjects: LCSH: Sponges–Juvenile literature.
Classification: LCC QL371.6 .S76 2018 | DDC 593.4–dc23
LC record available at https://lccn.loc.gov/2017029008

Published in 2019 by
Gareth Stevens Publishing
111 East 14th Street, Suite 349
New York, NY 10003

Designer: Andrea Davison-Bartolotta and Laura Bowen
Editor: Joan Stoltman

Photo credits: Cover, p. 1 ullstein bild/Getty Images; pp. 2–24 (background) Dmitrieva Olga/Shutterstock.com; p. 5 (top left, bottom left) Jolanta Wojcicka/Shutterstock.com; p. 5 (top right) Tom Goaz/Shutterstock.com; pp. 5 (bottom right), 9 Seaphotoart/ Shutterstock.com; p. 7 Colin Keates/Dorling Kindersley/Getty Images; p. 11 (main) SARAWUT KUNDEJ/Shutterstock.com; p. 13 ullstein bild/Getty Images; p. 15 Norbert Wu/ Minden Pictures/Getty Images; p. 17 Courtesy of NOAA; p. 19 Jeff Rotman/Photolibrary/ Getty Images; p. 21 photobynorman/Shutterstock.com.

Printed in the United States of America

CPSIA compliance information: Batch #CS18GS: For further information contact Gareth Stevens, New York, New York at 1-800-542-2595.

CONTENTS

Boldface words appear in the glossary.

Are Sponges Animals?

You may not think of sponges as animals. They don't have arms, eyes, mouths, or many other parts most animals have. For years, people even thought they were plants! But just like other animals, they eat, try to stay safe, and need **oxygen**!

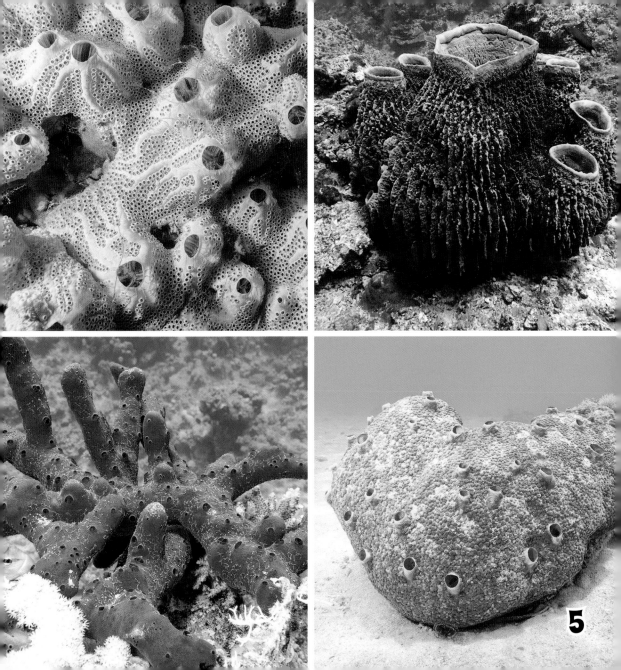
5

Earth's First Animal

Sponges are the oldest animals on Earth! Sponge **fossils** that are 600 million to 650 million years old have been found! Their body hasn't changed much since then. It seems that sponges have always had a soft body covered in a hard **layer** with many holes.

SPONGE FOSSIL

Fossils show that sponges have always lived in every ocean in both warm and cold water. They still do today! One reason they've been around so long is because they **reproduce** in several ways. Some sponges can even grow from a piece of broken sponge!

9

A Day in the Life

There are around 5,000 kinds of sponge with bodies of all sorts of shapes, colors, and **textures**. Most sponges are 0.4 inch to 120 inches (1 to 305 cm) tall. They all live the same way, though! Sponges spend every minute sucking in, **filtering**, and pushing out water!

A Long, Long Life

There are many guesses about how long sponges live. The ways used to tell how old something is don't work on sponges. Some could live for 1,000 years! A sponge in the East China Sea may even be 11,000 years old!

CARIBBEA
SEA SPONGE

13

Another sponge near Antarctica may be even older! It's hard to guess the age of Antarctic sea life. The cold and ice make these waters hard to **explore**. Plus, many things grow larger near the poles than in the rest of the world.

In 2015, a sponge the size of a minivan was found off the coast of Hawaii. It grew in an **ecosystem** people take special care of, which might be how it was able to get so big! It was 11.5 feet (3.5 m) long!

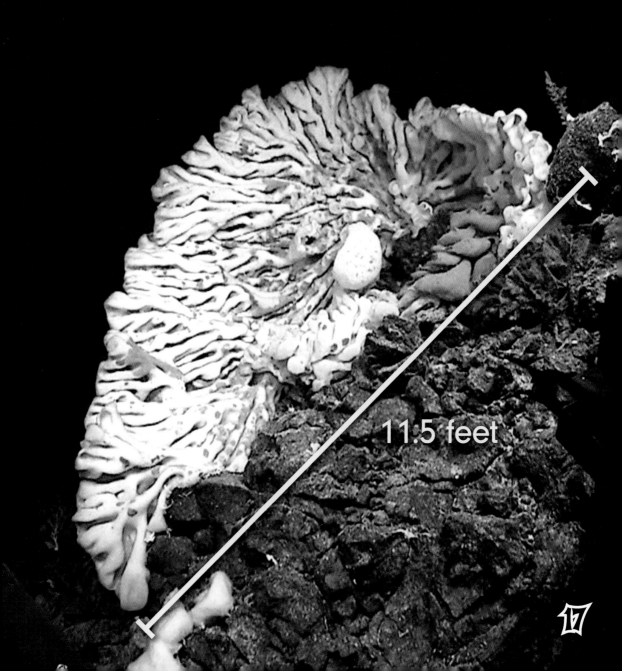
11.5 feet

Save the Sponges!

Most of Earth is deep under the ocean, and it's never been explored! The old sponges and sponge fossils in this book have all been discovered in the past few years because of new tools. Finally, we can see what's in the deep sea!

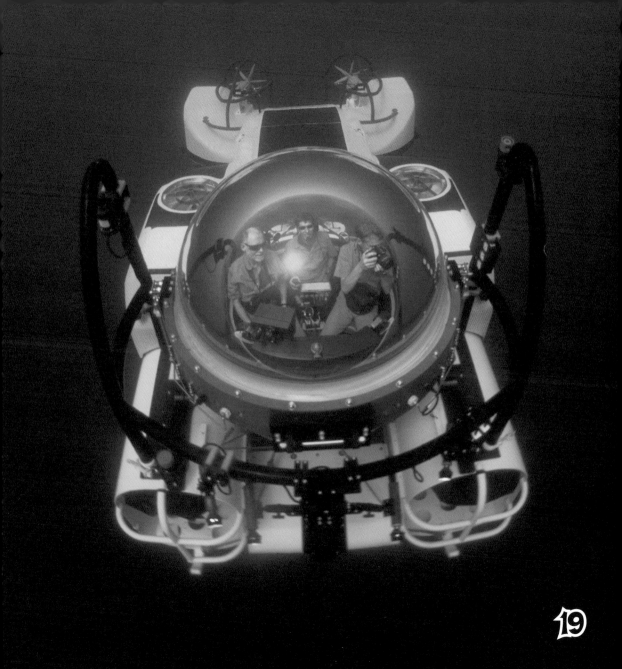

Though there's a lot we don't know, we do know sponges are great for their ecosystem! Many animals live safely inside sponges, plus sponges keep the water clean. Because they grow slowly, sponges need clean oceans to be the world's longest-living animals!

21

GLOSSARY

ecosystem: all the living things in an area

explore: to search in order to find out new things

filter: to collect bits from a liquid passing through

fossil: the hardened remains of a plant or animal that lived long ago

layer: one thickness of something lying over or under another

oxygen: a gas found in the air that has no color, taste, or smell, and that is needed for life

reproduce: when an animal creates another creature just like itself

texture: the structure, feel, and appearance of something

FOR MORE INFORMATION

BOOKS

Lunis, Natalie. *Squishy Sponges*. New York, NY: Bearport Publishing Company, Inc., 2017.

Magby, Meryl. *Sponges*. New York, NY: PowerKids Press, 2013.

Sexton, Colleen. *Sponges*. Minneapolis, MN: Bellwether Media, 2010.

WEBSITES

Phylum Porifera
ryanphotographic.com/sponges.htm
There are so many beautiful photos of colorful sponges to see here!

Sponge Species
flowergarden.noaa.gov/about/spongelist.html
Check out these beautiful pictures of all sorts of sponges.

Publisher's note to educators and parents: Our editors have carefully reviewed these websites to ensure that they are suitable for students. Many websites change frequently, however, and we cannot guarantee that a site's future contents will continue to meet our high standards of quality and educational value. Be advised that students should be closely supervised whenever they access the Internet.

INDEX